T'was the Dawn Before Christmas . . .

based on
Luke 1:26-35; 2:1-20

by
Robert & Alice Lewis

endurancepress

T'was the Dawn before Christmas...
is available at special quantity discounts for bulk purchase for sales promotions,
premiums, fund-raising, and educational needs.
For details write Endurance Press, 577 N Cardigan Ave Star, ID 83669.

Visit Endurance Press' website at www.endurancepress.com

T'was the Dawn before Christmas...

PUBLISHED BY ENDURANCE PRESS
577 N Cardigan Ave
Star, ID 83669 U.S.A.

Cover art by Robert Lewis
Author Photo credit Lewis Family Photo's.

Interior artwork credit Robert Lewis

ISBN 978-0-9964975-5-8

Cover Design by Teal Rose Design Studio's

Printed in the United States of America

First Edition 2016

T'was the Dawn before Christmas,

the angel Gabriel came to Galilee,

To deliver a message

to the Virgin Mary.

Joseph left the city where he and Mary abided.

Going to Bethlehem where they were guided...

From Nazareth to Bethlehem

they needed to go.

Though the road was
well-traveled,

the going was slow.

8

They journeyed with trembling to the city of Bread,
that would be the Son's birthplace as the Scriptures
had said.

The journey was long and hard.
They traveled with caution and care.
For Mary was with child, and soon she would bear.

Upon their arrival, weary within,
they looked for shelter, but found
no room in the inn.

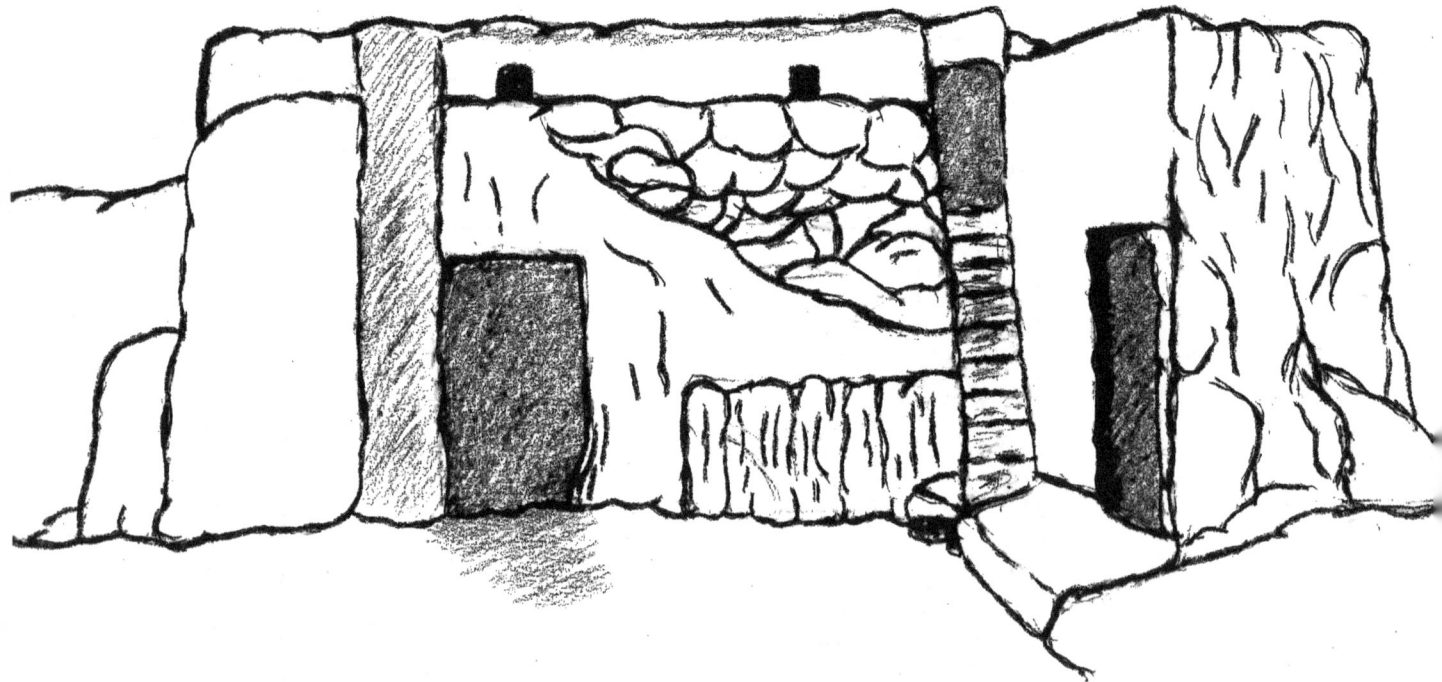

Sent to a stable filled with animals and hay.
A safe place was found for Mary to lay.

As she gave birth to Jesus
the holy Christ child.
The angel appeared to the shepherds
Proclaiming Him holy, meek, and mild!

Shepherds in the field
Watching their flock at night
Became very afraid
With the angel shining bright.

He said to them all. With a very great shout!
"Good tidings of great joy to all round about."

In the city of David
born on this day...
is Christ the Lord,
The Savior, the Way!

You will find in a manger in a stable nearby,
wrapped in swaddling clothes the Christ child shall lie.

16

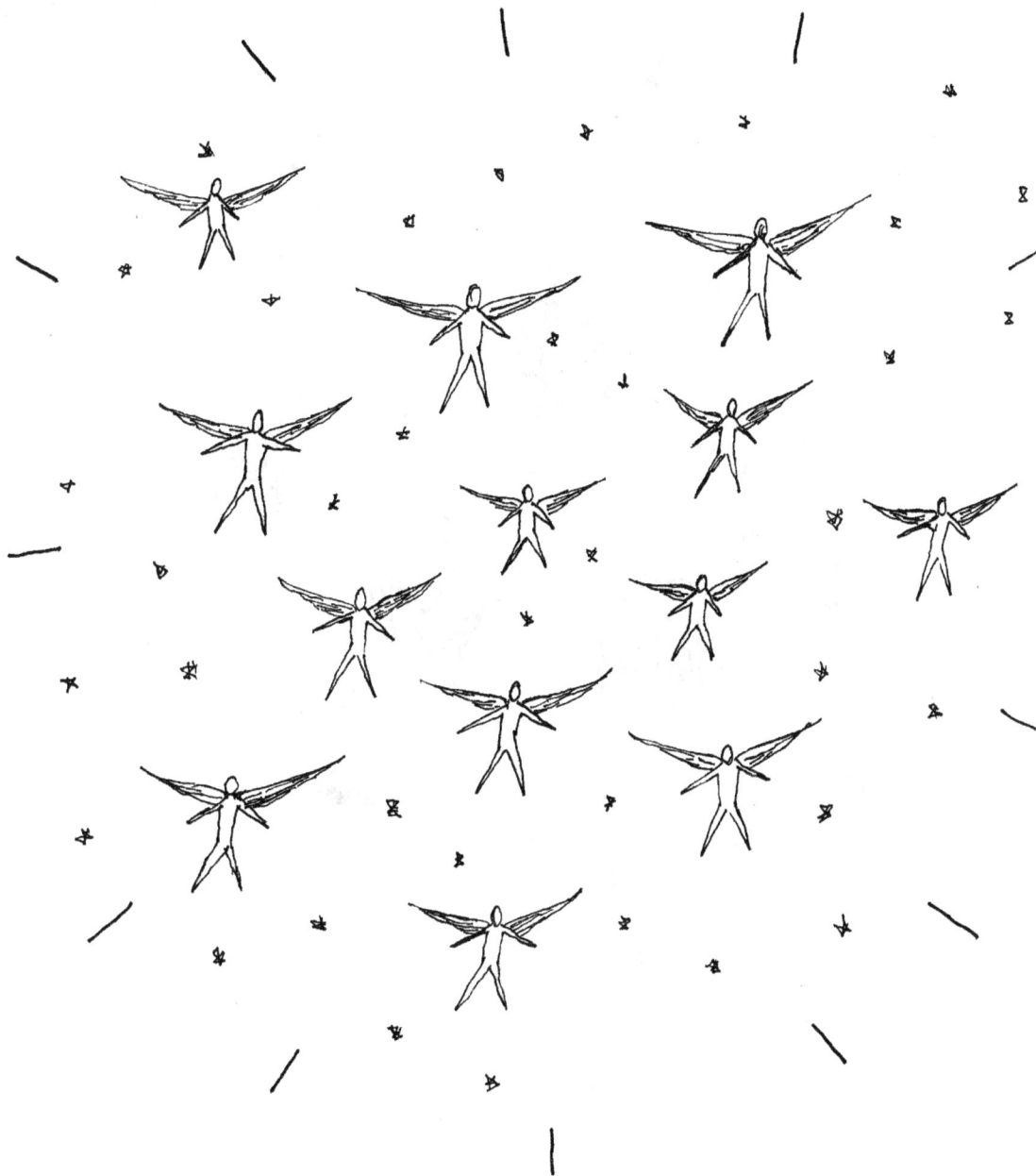

Then suddenly in the night sky many angels appeared.
All praising God with this message to hear.

Glory to God in the highest, at the Great Redeemer's birth!

Great kindness to all let there be peace on earth!

18

When the angels departed the shepherds all said.
"Let's go to Bethlehem that great house of Bread."

We want to see for ourselves
What has come to pass
What the Lord has made known
20   So they made haste to get there fast!

They found Mary and Joseph after they arrived,
and baby Jesus in a manger where softly He cried.

They spread the word around concerning this baby, this
child. And everyone that heard it wondered awhile!
Who was this baby? And what would He be?
Only in time will they all finally see!

With their hearts filled with joy for the news spread abroad, to their fields the shepherds all went shouting praises and glorifying God!

For a Child was borne, a Son was given.
He is Christ, the Lord, the Savior from Heaven!

www.ingramcontent.com/pod-product-compliance
Lightning Source LLC
Chambersburg PA
CBHW081235020426
42331CB00012B/3190